TWISTED SPIRITUAL POETRY

CHARLES BATEMAN

Copyright @2021 by Charles Bateman

All rights reserved. No part of this book may be reproduced in any form or by any electronic or mechanical means, including information storage and retrieval systems, without permission in writing from the publisher, except by reviewers, who may quote brief passages in a review.

This publication contains the opinions and ideas of its author. It is intended to provide helpful and informative material on the subjects addressed in the publication. The author and publisher specifically disclaim all responsibility for any liability, loss or risk, personal or otherwise, which is incurred as a consequence, directly or indirectly, of the use and application of any of the contents of this book.

WORKBOOK PRESS LLC
187 E Warm Springs Rd,
Suite B285, Las Vegas, NV 89119, USA

Website: https://workbookpress.com/
Hotline: 1-888-818-4856
Email: admin@workbookpress.com

Ordering Information:
Quantity sales. Special discounts are available on quantity purchases by corporations, associations, and others. For details, contact the publisher at the address above.

ISBN-13:   978-1-954753-40-2 (Paperback Version)
                978-1-954753-41-9 (Digital Version)

REV. DATE: 22.02.2021

ACKNOWLEDGEMENT

My deepest appreciation to....

All those who encouraged me and helped me in prayer, project, and financial support to brink this book to completion; to Chareese, a magnificent best friend of mine.

I want to thank also my brother; Robert and sister-in-law Denise, this book would not be complete without you.

Most importantly, my gratitude to the Lord and Savior Jesus for His grace and companionship during this project and the Holy Spirit's faithful guidance through this assignment.

DEDICATION

I dedicate this book to the memory of my mother and my sister Debbie, my subrino Paul Aspacio, my brothers Clark, John, and Robert and my daughter Raquel.

This book is about healing broken hearts, encouraging those who feel hopeless and giving to the needy.

NO MORE

Telling my story is so hard to do, the pain is so hard to bare, there is much I confess was a terrible mess, to what of it can I compare? there is so much you see?

So unsettled in me I would look out my window and stare. I had my first drink at age seven, I smoked my first bong hit at nine, at age fourteen I overdosed on tequila, I drank so much that I nearly died. From there my life seemed so confusing, I hardly knew what to do with my time, so I just kept on using to forget about this life of mine.

I lost every job that they gave me, I drank until I was a corpse, once I even went to Las Vegas and bet on a high loosing horse.

In the eighties things just got harder as I got addicted to meth, my skin literally crawled as I stood by the wall and I prayed for a slow painful death. Now I've put it behind me, now I'm finally clean, it's been three years in the making with no more of that life for me.

MY WORLD

In the deepest, darkest of night you have invaded my dream.

Your ruby lips are full , beautiful pillows that when kissed by them I am set on fire.

You must know that in that heat, that one simple act my blood boils over consumed by your juices forcing me to swallow every drop.

No other woman could take your place for you have branded my ass with your name and I will always be ready to make sweet, hard love with no interruptions, for I long to inhale every part of you , my lover, my mate, my world.

BETTER THAN

Better a small hut with peace and quiet than a mansion full of feasting and selfish gain for too much of that will drive you insane.

Better to live alone than to be with the one that you despise, you can see her contempt in her hideous eye's.

Better to be poor and debt free than to have it all without peace of mind.

Better to give and receive for to go without one or the other is not wise.

Better to forgive than to harbor a grudge why die before your time

Better to love than to hate for hatred is like poison which will destroy a righteous man .

Better to die than to be born for birth is the beginning of woe's.

MY OWN WAY

No man has ever had knowledge of you, your virginity is a well-kept secret.

Many men have pursued you only to find they were not worthy of your treasure.

I have only gazed upon your beauty from afar, In the night I dreamed an unholy dream, that one day I would ask for your hand in righteous matrimony.

For you I will move mountains, I will cross the oceans to find a vow I made in the dew drop morning, singing a song of true love for I must tell you that in the dead of night I caressed myself while thinking of you, please forgive my boldness as I was without control.

But now I resign myself to give way to a suiter much younger and more handsome than I, quietly, I go my own way.

There will be a time when we must choose between what is easy, and what is right.

—A. DUMBLEDORE

ONLY YOU

I dream in earnest about the curves of your frame, tantalizing is the scent of your well. your hair is long and is like an ocean wave that beckons my promise, you will never be nor should you ever be tamed.

As you are young, you are wild and you are free

to be the woman you desire to be. It's your free will that draws me in as many a men have tried but failed to see your mind, your heart and your soul. that is my wealth, my passion and my birth right to love only you.

FOR YOU

Do you feel like your drifting? like doves gliding on the breeze? You feel so high as your kissing the sky and it brings you down to your knees.

Here there is nothing to be afraid of, here the lion lays with the lambs, how much love and respect do I dish out? 7.70 x70 grams.

For you see I love without limits, I 've learned to forgive every wrong, in our hearts we can be without hatred, we can all just get along.

In this world we will have trials, in this world we will know pain, love each person as we want to be loved again, again, and again. I am going to do my part as my higher power shows me to do, when it's all said and done both the work and the fun I'll be waiting in heaven for you.

MASKS

Drowning in sorrow, I walk with a cane, it's real complicated but I'll try to explain. When I was a child, the masks that were worn were there to protect me since the day I was born.

I had a mother and a father you see, but that didn't stop the beatings on me. I had nobody, I had not one friend, in school I was bullied and harassed without end.

I prayed to Jesus but he never came, my teachers ignored me they added to my shame. This is my story. I tell it with care, why did this happen? why is life so unfair?

There are other children whom have it harder than me, they hope for redemption, and a chance to be free.

Now I am older, and so blessed to be, now I have friends who share their love and it's free, no more beatings but I still wear a mask, I'll take it off if politely you ask.

DYING WISH

Sunlight glistening waves crashing down, living waters, you shall thirst no more. Inner beauty without blemish unflawed. Love unrequited is thigh reward.

A beating heart living long in your disdain, yours is a tumultuous companion, seek thee a dry quiet plain and there find your peace, not undone but complete without end for without it we are destined to die and whom will come?

No my friend, this will not be your story, you will sprout wings of an angel then? Just fly.

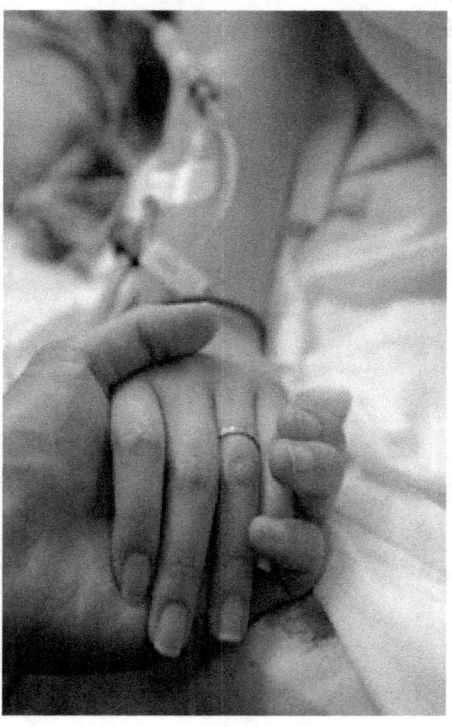

DONE

In your hollow eyes is the story I seek, I may write in a day, or it might take a week. I'll start with the way you snatched all that I owned, my heart, my soul, my skin and my bone, you then took my feelings, you trampled them good the damage so hard to repair.

I sat in our room with a heart full of gloom, the sign on our wall read beware.

Who could I turn to? what could I do? as I sat on the porch and I wept. I had no friends that's the way that it ends.

I only had peace when I slept. I made up my mind I would never again get with a woman like you, you make my skin itch, you're a low bottom bitch, I'm thankful we're finally through.

THOSE SHOES

To many times did I trust you every chance that I gave you bereaved , for hours I stood in the pouring rain with my feelings all over my sleeve .

You were cold blooded and evil , what you did in secret was known, your cheating way, at the end of the day was the only thing that you owned .

Your smile was just a distraction, your well to do mask just a ploy, the game that you played, smoking meth in the shade robbed me of all of my joy.

I was the hopeless shell of a man, desperate and infested with hate, while you popped pills with your friend, I was right near the end, sitting outside by the gate.

Now the table is turned, now I am so rid of you, your weak little mind is not much of a find, no longer do I walk in those shoes.

SO THANKFUL

I stand in front of a big white page I stand alone but I'm not forgotten, those that remember the days of old the memories are decayed and rotten.

Me? I'm older and the lessons. I've learned are riding upon my shoulders, the fire I breath, the lies that I weave warm me as the nights here grow colder.

I'm not a robot nor am I a machine I can feel every insult you throw me, You see?

I am free it's the best way to be, if you think I am wrong, simply show me.

For paragraph 2 there is so much to do, I may need someone to help me, no one shallow nor plain there is so much to gain and you stretched out your hand then you felt me.

Here we reside with our flaws we denied because the truth is always so painful, the lie I confess in this terrible mess is forgotten and I am so thankful.

GOODNIGHT

In my mind are wonders that the eye can't see, a wide array of fractals that dwell inside of me. Mountain tops and plush green valley's rule the opened plains, countless flowers are everywhere I washed out all the stains.

Here you won't find negative thoughts but you will need a key, I cannot let just anyone in that may be a threat to me.

Fluffy pillows and clean white sheets when it's time for bed, puppy dog pets and no regrets are swimming in my head.

Here it's always summer but first it's always spring, wonderful sounds echo through the air you can hear the angels sing, no bad dreams nor nightmares only what's good and right, until we meet again my friends I bid you all good night.

MENTAL

So here we are in the middle of winter I hunger for the spring, I take 60 mgs of Adderall, grab my guitar and I sing.

For depression I take 40 mgs of Prozac to keep me off the edge, suicide is not an option, get that right through my head.

I am a master of mental disorders bi polar through and through, it's just a fact but I am not wacked I'm just telling you the truth.

I never get angry nor justify my actions when I know I am wrong, lets live in peace and harmony why can't we just get along?

ONLY A TEST

The tiles are missing from the kitchen floor and there are no pellets for the stove, there is no heat nor warmth to cover me, no blankets did she wove.

Time just smiles and mocks my pain, it really could care less, nothing to do but count the beats deep inside my chest. Are there no visitors? Who will come? Does anybody care?

I mark the notches on my wall with a cold unloving stare. Now it's time, make a choice, if I really want to be free, what is needed deep down below is a lock without a key.

This is the thing all good poets simply need to know, is how to move and manipulate words in every single row. This is it, the very last sentence, I hope you all the best.

I'm cutting the line, with no fish to find, it's only been a test.

JUST A THOUGHT

I search high and low, looking for truth in the innermost parts, my mind is a spiral stair case. Where I file my thoughts and store all of my dreams.

High and mighty in my mind I am king, searching for solace in a vast network of pods, nooks, and crannies.

In my travels I meet attitudes seemingly, without any emotion, perched above the latitude are vertical dwellings unfit for occupation, so they to this day are just empty shells waiting to be invaded.

Stop! for the road ahead has been washed away, forcing all to find another way back home.

UNEVOLVING

I sit in my post-apocalyptic waste land pondering the ways of the world, a baby stroller blocks the entrance to a once inhabited night club, no more are there the sounds of people celebrating what at one time was life.

Degradation, Oprah Winfrey, Helen DeGeneres memories of better days, now there is famine, children are eating the ashes from old bomb debris, ladders only go down never up, welcome to the age of nuclear fallout, it's called that because it does make your hair fall out.

An alien is running the show claiming to be God but!!! he is an imposter handing out animal balloons.

Nobody is actually breathing as they are half dead half alive creatures of the night, smoking meth, drinking bathtub gin, grumbling and complaining because there just, isn't, anything else to do. farewell my friends it's been, interesting, ciao.

PERFECT PEACE

I stand alone against an army, I stand in line my turn to die, I muster all my faith and courage without ever asking why.

There are many in the valley, there they wait to decide, they don't know that they are warriors, in God's power they do abide.

In the clouds God's mighty army, that are with the one afraid, I can count at least one legion, many ran but one man stayed.

It's never too late to be forgiven for the prince of peace is here, just say a simple prayer to Jesus he is always standing near.

Lord forgive me my heart is heavy, all weighed down with sin and grief, I lay my all at your feet Lord, all my sins for perfect peace.

LIFE? OR DEATH?

How can truth be shared in this apocalyptic waste land? and why are the masses so offended by it? it all comes down to what we see, and what we feel.

I am living proof that a being far greater than I molded and shaped me, at times he chipped away useless fragments that did me no earthly good and still what this being adds is far better than what he removes.

My friends the tree of life is far healthier than the tree of knowledge, In the end the choice is yours. Life? or death?

IN TIME

As I travel on this path, narrow is the way.

My companion's pain and suffering, the woes are here to stay.

They are not to be compared with the glory which lay ahead, for there I'll bask in perfect peace with a crown upon my head.

To all of you I say take your place in heaven up above, there we will walk on streets of gold cast into his perfect love.

This is what I need to know when fear and doubt creep in, he gave his life upon that cross, I gave him my sin. So if you find your running low I know how you feel, take it easy as you go in time your wounds will heal.

COVID FROM CHINA TO US

The tide is slowly rising, death is in the air, traffic comes to an overly crowded highway now a congested and endless mess. Who is my enemy? What does he hope to gain as the platform twists and turns to an unwanted guest?

I'm going down into the depths. I'm going to murder anyone that stands in my way, evil man beware because you don't want to be on the receiving end of my wrath, because of you we're chocking and spewing out the toxic air you brought upon this our free soil and it shall forever remain free of your communist intent.

When the shit hits the fan I wouldn't want to be you. This is our sacred ground, tread softly for you tread on my values, my desires and my dreams, these will be the boundaries we set for you as we march you back to the rock you crawled out from.

We shall never conform to your ways; this is my putting you on notice! deal with it bitch.

BRING HELL TO AN END

Dear God, I approach you as a humble friend, I ask you to please bring hell to an end, the thief's the liars the suicides, please let them with you abide.

Lord forgive me I ask so much, have mercy on those whom suffer such.

I am certain they've learned their lesson there bring hell to an end it's only fair, there must be something you can do, nothing is too big for you.

Lord, I beg thee this poem I send, Lord please bring hell to an end.

Lord everyone there knows the score, shut it down and bolt the door. I have to ask you once again, Lord please!! bring hell to an end.

YOU

You must know that your special. there is no other like you, your giving and kind, your one heck of a find no other description will do.

I've watched you very carefully, sometimes you give till it hurts. You worry and fret and you count your regrets and wonder if you have any worth.

I am here to tell you your value is more precious than gold, and the lies you believed as you were being deceived are dying, crippled and old.

It's time to put down the hammer, your heart is beat up black and blue, it's time to heal as you learn how to feel, you see I need to learn these things too.

MY POINT OF VIEW

Long and wide is the road to hell, many there be that find it.

The devil promised them riches and fame, with a contract and they up and signed it.

Some believe that hell is the world, their sorrows are many to be counted, if you come across a bag full of woe's, leave that shit where you found it.

I'm just a spectator leaving my mark in a world full of grave confusion, the grass being greener on the other side of town is just a grand illusion.

I'm certain of many things' that this life has taught me, when I was falling, spiraling out of control Jesus reached out his hand and he caught me. All of you have value and worth, if your struggling my friend's just hang in there, I assume that you know the rest, I believe life can be fair.

WALK ON

Life is here but for only the living, are you trapped in the dark never giving? Are you down for the challenge that I'm bringing before you? In my heart I love and adore you.

Mesmerized by the way that I say it, if you're playing a game then go on and play it.

The merry-go-round that you ride around there, has to stop no one said life would be fair. I'm writing about what this ugly world up and gave me, not once did anyone offer to save me.

It's not a resentment, I hold no grudges I'm not the stubborn mule that never budges.

Now I'm in the mix, I got that paper, I picked up the love and I put down the razor.

These days' I am loved, that is my treasure, this is my gift of significant measure.

The day's turn to night so I'll leave the light on, now you're a man and it's time to walk-on.

BREATHE

I dread the day, wrapped around my neck the taker's come out to play, stealing statues from their neighbor's yard's, they tell you they bought them at Walmart.

Their lives are made up of routine's, they come and they go never finding a quiet place to lay their heads.

I too at one time did follow a crowd of people that stole my self-respect.

What will I gain by hating those that found amusement as I coiled up like an infant going through with-drawls.

It's an uncertain life as I traded my soul for a drug that took away my pain, be it for just a little while, that is all I wanted, it was the only solace I could find.

Those that used me and loaded me with guilt as many-a-time I tried to run away, but I had nowhere to go.

Today I am a free man, those that hurt me are in my rear view mirror, now? I can breathe.

KEEP YOUR FEET DRY AND CLEAN

I've been in a funk and it's cramping my style someone please come feed the beast, on my neck he is breathing his anger is seething, he thought he would dine on a feast.

My mind is made up, I'm pissed off and fed up, if he move's just one more inch, I gave him fare warning, I'll be glad in the morning and be rid of his foul smelling stench.

In this life we have choices we just need use our voices and sometimes we might make a scene, do what you must, leave your foe's in the dust, in the end keep your feet dry and clean.

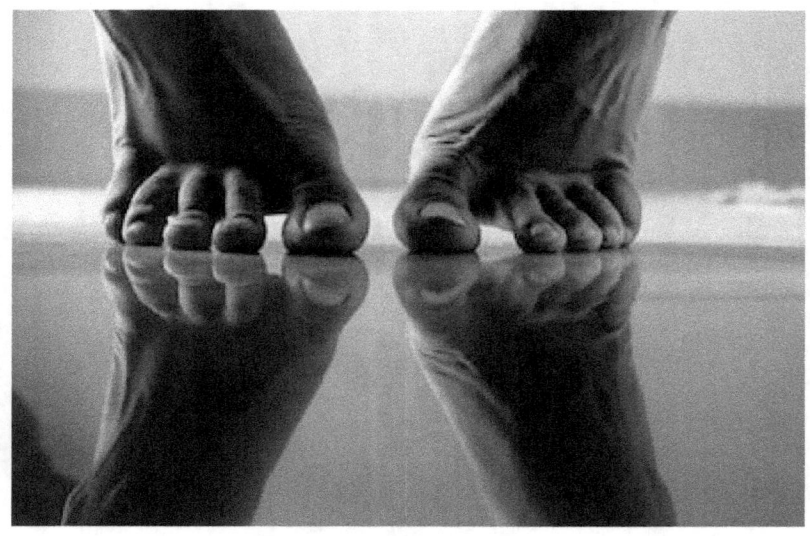

FIGHT TO GIVE

We're like dog's in a corner itching to bite, when push comes to shove we are in for a fight.

This is the way I feel it needs to be, we have to throw punches if we want to be free.

When the fighting is over, it's time for peace, it's the way I prefer to say the least.

It's been said love thy neighbor as we want to be loved, my friend's we can do this with help from above.

Please know as you read this it's a good way to live, don't be a taker and learn how to give.

In all of my years I've come to believe, it's better to give than it is to receive.

I'll leave this impression and you can be the judge, how much should we give? what we have is enough.

PUT DOWN YOUR GUN

I'm having a hard time, I'm failing to see, late is the hour for you and for me.

As for what to write I've made a list, punching my pillow with the ball of my fist.

I will be candid, I'll make it clear, not knowing what come's next is the what' that I fear.

We all of us have value, all of us have worth, we all begin dying at the time of our birth. Rhadamanthine, now there's a big word, it mean's incorruptible and a chance to be heard.

So I will forge a new iron I will lead without fear, because I know how to follow so be of good cheer. When it's all over, all said and done, pick up the love and put down your gun.

MY LIFE

My life has been a long winding road, lonely and tired no sympathy showed.

I hold to no grudges , no resentments nor hate , I've learned some hard lessons the first? was to wait.

In this life of trials I seldom did know , the love of a father and onward I go.

Still I'm no sceptic, it's plain to see? the scars on this heart beating inside of me.

They are not random, I know every one, each has a name, the damage is done.

Now I am older, wiser for the wear, I look to the future with a thousand-yard stare. one more round for the end of the show, the cuts come quickly but the healing is slow.

KNEEL

The still morning slumber, the thousand-yard stare, the children eat ashes but why should we care?

The mephitic bodies lye dead on the floor, ten to a pile we make room for more.

Repine by nature, why shouldn't we be. we open our eye's still we're to blind to see.

To the lost and those hurting that need to be heard, to offer them healing and a couple kind words.

So kneel at the altar, acknowledge your shame, brother forgive me and I'll do the same.

THE DEFINITION OF US

My mind is a spiral stair case and there you just might see , that I am just like one of you , and you are just like me .

I've been told that I look angry , the dent between my eye's , it came from years of public abuse and cut me down to size.

Still I just keep trying and I will never quit, because the role of this old soul is no stranger to the shit. If you have seen what I've seen, to what can I compare?

P T S D for you and for me and the one hundred-thousand-yard stare.

So, we shall keep on trying and we shall never quit, instead we'll fly thru the clear blue skies and keep our candles lit.

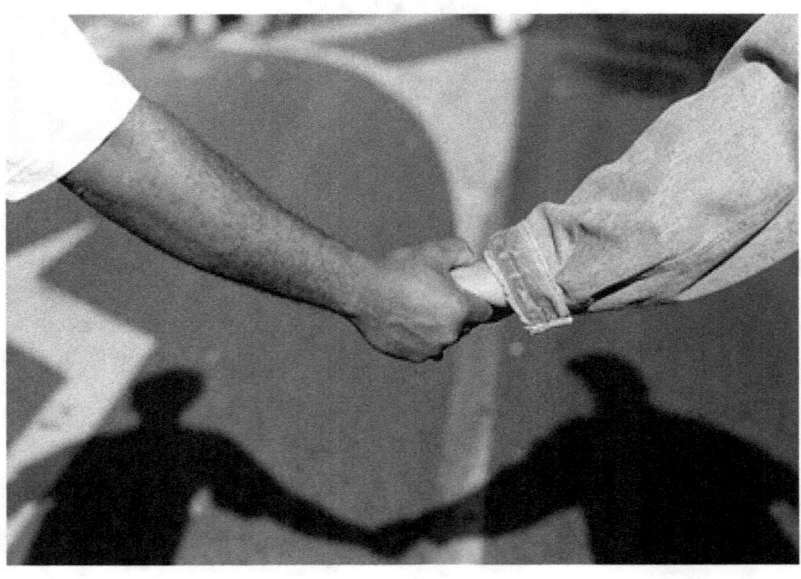

FREE

The jagged edge of a single thought will rip open the flesh, unrelenting agony at the hands of a heart breaker.

I search my soul at the inner most parts, truth unfolds hardly making a sound, lie's to pass the time, ugly is your deceit.

Your reward shall be utter torment for you would not suffer me to weep as I lost all that I love. Oh my soul why are you down cast?

You have never known the warmth of true love, you struggle as a fish in a net.

When will I be shown mercy? Where is my portion of bread?

I will not eat it for it is full of discontent, I will not drink the blood of wrath which is given without mixture, but here I sit and wait to be free.

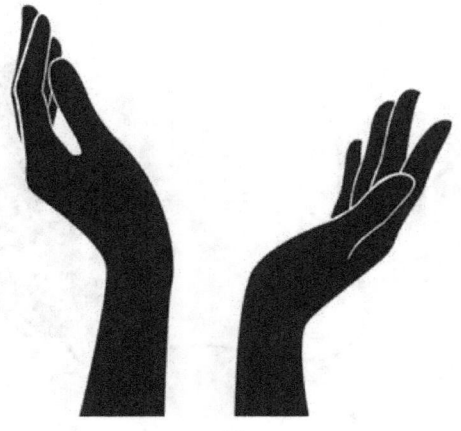

PIT IT ALL BY EAR

As I rage on in this world hard and cold it's not growing old that I fear, it's not knowing my way, should I go? or just stay I play it all by ear.

You tighten your grip around my throat but it's not death that I fear ,
loosing again I just bare it and grin, I play it all by ear.

I lost all my fight I feel tired in the night ,the setting foreboding and queer ,remember my name while you're playing your game , I play it all by ear.

You took everything from me , your callous and mean so what are you doing here ? I took it all back your fat lying sack, because I play it all by ear.

GENUINE

If you think that I can't write poems like this, I fully understand,
to find the right words a tedious challenge but on the other hand.
The reason that I do this, with the clutter in my mind,
at times I'm only venting, not meant to be unkind.
I do it to feel like I belong, don't mistake me for weak,
I am not a carnival worker, or a 40's circus freak.
Be careful how you judge me, for I am just like you,
A starving poet whom loves to write I have to see it through.
This one is finally over so I'll leave you with this,
clap your hands, with no demands and blow my ass a kiss !!

GRACE

I've been down to hell below , third seat to the right the second row ,

old friends were in torment crying out for mercy.

I was there a frightened man , my legs were to weak I couldn't

stand I thought that I was condemned and left to suffer.

All of the sudden I saw a light it was radiant and so was I ,

the peace that I felt just blew me away in that moment.

So if your lost cry out his name , he won't judge you nor will he cast any blame , all of your sins and wrong doings can be forgiven.

he knows your struggling , inside you're a mess , he sees your heart hurting inside your chest , one at a time he will heal all cuts and bruises.

So when your questioning your motives and faith, you need to make some room on your plate, his love is always there for those that choose it.

EPHESIANS 2:8

HIS FACE

I have seen the most beautiful face, glowing with compassion ,

mercy and grace.

I could see he has power to forgive every sin ,I was just blown

away as I invited him in.

The love unlike anything I have known,

ever so humble with a spiritual tone he took a beating because of men and their laws , willingly he did this, he believed in his cause.

Someday we will see the whole, heavy, cost, the day he was nailed to that old rugged cross and I will remember his face forever.

CRASH

Ever so gently your loving embrace engulfs me your sweet breath is an opiate high

swimming in your waters, your scent drives me into a frenzy.

I will drink from your well alone for a vow was made

I will meet your breast with a gentile caress ever so lightly I feel the slip of your earlobe between my lips as I lay next to your curves I lovingly kiss the nape of yourneck.

softly whispering my love for you and only you.

TRUTH

The truth is untarnished, the truth never lies, it needs no excuses or cheap alibis.

The truth will expose every deed that is done, for the thief and the liar it's a hot smoking gun.

the truth will set free those wrongly accused , the truth always knows when it's just being used .

the truth can be a companion and friend , or it can come crashing down and bring it all to an end.

So, search the truth in your heart and you just might see, that you have been hurt and abused but now the truth set you free.

MAN IN NEED

The woes of a poor man are only counted by him

His empty pockets constantly remind him of his plight in his world he hasn't a well to draw from who will help him in his time of need?

Remember when you also were in tatters , you held out your hand and received your portion

consider the poor man's needs above your own and discover your humanity and give.

ONE THOUSAND FACES

I cannot draw pictures but if I could , I would draw every detail be they proper and good.

You would be amazed as you get lost in each curve, the bitter church lady would yell , you have some nerve !!!

But as it stands a face I can't draw , instead I write letters, if you read them all?

You may see faces , mountains and trees , or someone that is dying from an unchecked disease.

Words retain power and the ones that I write paint one thousand faces when their read in the light.

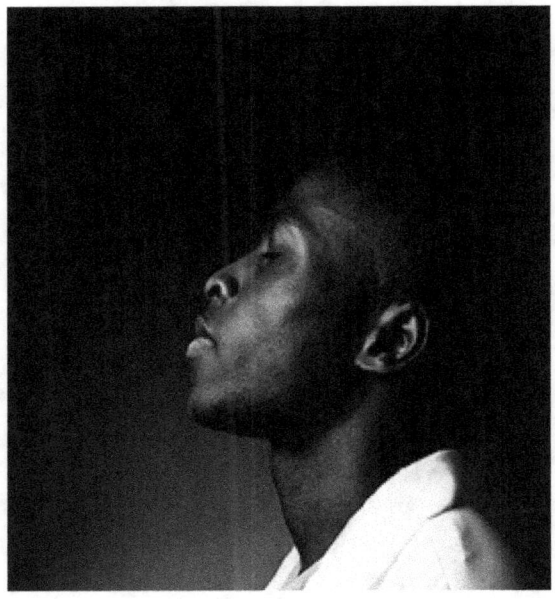

INSPIRE

I will never judge you with hatred or disdain,

I will never cause you strife that you may in peace remain.

God forbid anyone insult you or clip your angel wings, I will stand in awe of you and the wonder that you bring.

I will knock down all the walls and break the lock on the door.

I will help you take the leap and watch your spirit soar for you I wrote this insignificant poem to tell you of your worth you will have your portion and your cup , you will be my friend secure.

EIGHT

Do not be relaxed, be on your guard, do not be a fool. for when we give in to strong drink we sin and the demons sit laughing and drool.

In darkness we're lost such a steep heavy cost the rips and the tares hard to mend, so come to the light you may have to fight but I will fight with you my friend.

SHAMELESS

The pain you try to cover up deep inside your heart, the abuse that you endured just ripped your world apart.

The anger that you cannot shake however hard you try.

Day by day it eats at you but doesn't tell you why.

Every day you mask your hurt afraid that someone just might see, I'm here to tell you Jesus does and longs to set you free.

Whatever it was that happened, you are not to blame, the source of your unhappiness, your ill unwanted shame.

Gently kneel and bow your head, open up your heart.

You don't have to change a thing Jesus loves you just the way that you are.

WISDOM

The roads may be long and the mountains are steep, we pay a price for the company we keep.

The lessons we learn lined with sorrow and pain, we wonder if we'll ever be happy again.

you've been gone for a while the prodigal son, your inheritance spent and your heart weighs a ton.

But the father rejoiced when he noticed his child, his arms opened wide in his forgive my son style.

You see your place in his kingdom was there all along you may have thought he'd be angry, thank God you were wrong.

*************** END *****************

www.ingramcontent.com/pod-product-compliance
Lightning Source LLC
Chambersburg PA
CBHW072039080526
44578CB00007B/533